Anonymous

The People's Answer to the Court Pamphlet

Entitled a Short Review of the Political State of Great Britain

Anonymous

The People's Answer to the Court Pamphlet
Entitled a Short Review of the Political State of Great Britain

ISBN/EAN: 9783337091859

Printed in Europe, USA, Canada, Australia, Japan

Cover: Foto ©Suzi / pixelio.de

More available books at **www.hansebooks.com**

THE

PEOPLE'S ANSWER

TO THE

COURT PAMPHLET:

ENTITLED

A SHORT REVIEW

OF THE

POLITICAL STATE OF GREAT BRITAIN.

Quid prius dicam SOLITIS Parentis
Laudibus? - - - - -

Printed for J. DEBRETT, oppofite Burlington-houfe
Piccadilly.

MDCCLXXXVII.

THE

PEOPLE'S ANSWER

TO THE

COURT PAMPHLET.

WHEN a new face, a new carriage, a
new pl·y, a new poem, a new novel, or
even a new pamphlet appears; if the ftile
of the features, the pannels, the plot,
the verfification, the ftory, or the politics,

be

be really *new*; a thoufand bufy inquiries are inftantly on foot, to analyfe and to criticife its merits. But fo few are the claffics of the Court, in modern times, fo completely Bæotian are the talents that St. James's can boaft, that even a Charade from one of the *King's Friends* would excite more admiration than half a dozen Probationary Odes from Oppofition. The circle at the Levee, like the orbit of the *Georgium Sidus*, is fo diftant from the Sun of Wit, as fcarcely to admit its feebleft light, with difficulty partake its leaft animating ardour.

To this confirmed defperation of all *Courtly Genius* may in part be afcribed the eclat with which a Pamphlet, publifhed a few days ago, has been received by the dull defponding train of an unlettered Court. 'This *Review of Politics*, which,

" as

" as a ftranger, has been welcomed like a
" ftranger," may be confidered as a fort
of handy manual for the Levee ; a kind of
Almanac Royal, or Court Calendar for the
new year, lightly touching on the topicks
moft in vogue, and fketching out handy
fentences for the Lords of the Bedcham-
ber to retail, or the Maids of Honour to
fcribble on their fans. It has accordingly
been as much talked of, if not more, than
any other of the fafhionable novelties of
the hour. It has been mentioned oftener
than the neweft *vis-à-vis*, or the prettieft
drefs at the Birth Day. The Pages learn
to fpell in it—The Gentlemen Penfioners
and the Beef-eaters, get it read to them,
in the Guard Chamber—The Chaplains
in ordinary copy its ftile in their fermons
—The Laureat is to verfify it—The
Houfehold Apothecaries to quote it—and
Mrs. *Jane Moore* carefully to depofit it,

where

where the wildeſt truants, from Courtly Literature, muſt on certain occaſions be neceſſarily tempted to a curſory difcuſſion of it. In a word, an *arrêt* has iſſued from the Runners of the Court to have *The Review* as generally read, as the Forms of Prayer were for ſubduing America, or the Thankſgiving, for the Triumph of Providence over Margaret Nicholſon.

It is curious to inveſtigate the motives for thus generally circulating the little Pamphlet in queſtion; and, as a good many, who ſtill think for themſelves, are not convinced either of the truth of its aſſertions, or the juſtneſs of its reflections, it is but fair to offer their remarks upon both, and in a plain brief way to put in, *The People's Anſwer* to the *Court Pamph-let.*

In

In order, then, to give clearnefs to **the**
comment, it may be as well to prefix a
fketch of the text ; or, in other words, **to**
form a fort of outline and abftract of **the**
work itfelf, preliminary to the few obfervations that are to be made on it.

THE REVIEW (which, by the way,
even in its Title, pleafantly recalls the
fafe engagements, and pacific victories **of**
Wimbledon and Blackheath) is principally
taken up, in difcuffing the characters of
Eight very extraordinary Perfonages—Seven
of the Drama living—but one dead—a lot,
which as *The Review* fagacioufly and
deeply obferves, " No TALENTS CAN
" EXEMPT US FROM."

The order of the Literary Review is as
follows :—Firft, (" as on every principle
" of duty, it was natural to begin") no
lefs

lefs a perfonage than the Sovereign himfelf—Next (as on every view of policy it
was wife to proceed) the Prince—Thirdly,
Mr. Pitt, by way of Companion to the
firft—Fourthly, Mr. Fox, in equal aid of
the fecond—Fifthly, Lord North, with,
Sixthly, THE BODY (I mean the late King
of Pruffia)—a fallen Minifter and a dead
King forming a moft difinterefted Coalition
—Seventhly, Lord Rodney, bearing the St.
Euftatia treafure; and, laft, in clofe connection with his Lordfhip, the virtuous,
the amiable Mr. Haftings, difplaying the
Turban that Cheit Sing had humbly prof-
trated at his feet.—What a banquet for Critical tafte ! not indeed a numerous bill of fare
—but furely a collection of the rareft and moft
variegated Dainties. — Lord Caermarthen's
intended dinner could have fcarcely exhi-
bited a more motley affemblage in its
guefts ; nor is it often that a Speech of

Lord

Lord Abingdon's contains fo incongruous a meeting, in jarring tropes and contradictory metaphors.

But to purfue our fubject. In the difcuffion of thefe eight Characters, the grand prefiding principle is flattery to his Majefty—not a coarfe unwieldy Flattery, like a Flemifh painter with a daubing brufh, glaring colours, and a gaudy varnifh—but a graceful, referved adulation, of the Italian fchool ; fo artfully difpofing the lights, fo fkillfully blending the fhades, as to irradiate or obfcure, to decorate or difgrace, the portrait, that Fancy or Averfion admires or difapproves.

Two artifices of compofition peculiarly characterize the ftile,—mimick praife, and fictitious cenfure—the former ferves as a convenient fkreen for cautious malice—

the

the latter, as a useful veil for discreet adulation. Thus (it being no inconsiderable object in a Court Pamphlet, to traduce even Ministers to a degree that may remind them to whom they are to look up) just enough of half objections to Mr. Pitt's character are interspersed, to give relief to the mass of commendation. Not a word escapes of serious censure; not a syllable, from this impartial writer, of that memorable breach of positive and solemn declaration, " neither directly nor " indirectly to sanction or support the ap- " prehended dissolution of Parliament"— not a syllable of the boasted contempt of Mr. Jenkinson's influence, established as it is by Lord Hawksbury's Places and Peerage —not a syllable of repeated failures and augmented vanity—of Taxes, abandoned, yet defended--of Irish Propositions, or of English Fortifications.—Safer are the re-

approaches

proaches, and milder the invective, which the Courtly Pamphlet levels againſt the Miniſter of the day. In this impartial Portraiture, Mr. Pitt is merely drawn as an " *awkward, ungraceful, cold,* and " *ſtately*" * Gentleman ! Epithets, which, though heavy impeachments of his Dancing-maſter's abilities, are not very likely to irretrievably prejudice a Miniſter in the public opinion. Mr. Pitt is accuſed too, with rather ſome inconſiſtency, conſidering his " Atlantean ſhoulders,†" of *inſenſibility to the attractions of women.*‡ An apathy, which, however, the ladies may have completely retaliated on this cold contemner of their charms, is, ſo far from prejudicial to a great public Character, that, in fact, it is the ut-

* Review, page 28.
† Id.
‡ Review, page 24.

moſt

moſt poſſible advantage to obtain it, par-
ticularly in the Finance Line ; in as much
as it ſecures a calm, diſpaſſionate delibera-
tion for the important occupations of the
Treaſury ; where indeed a ſort of *natural
Abelard* is at all times the apteſt character
to preſide ; but more eſpecially at a period,
when not only the *puny** Lords, but even
both the Secretaries of that department are
known, either in the Gallant or the
Uxorious character, to waſte no incon-
ſiderable portion of their hours in all thoſe
gentle avocations, which blend raptures
with reports, and eſtimates with *billet
doux* ; to the great annoyance of all ſober
calculation, and the no ſmall diſcompoſure
of a truly temperate arithmetick.

To this ingenious duplicity, which flat-
ters under the maſque of Satire, the ſtile of

* Alii legunt *Puiſne.*

the

the *Court Pamphlet* combines as curious an hypocrify of a contrary kind; in panegy-rick that afperfes, and applaufe that ope-rates as traduction. Thus Mr. Fox is celebrated for " placability and a forgiving " difpofition," fo placable, as ftrangely to forget his paft enmity to Lord North; fo forgiving, as unaccountably to coalefce with thofe he formerly oppofed.—The difpofi-tion and the temper of benevolence are in theory applauded; in fpeculation moft no-ble: to bring them into action, and give reality to idea, is a practice wholly to be condemned. Mr. Fox's " boldnefs too, " and his decifion," are generoufly admit-ted—boldnefs, however, that was " en- " croachment on the Honour of the Crown;" decifion, " that proved temerity " in the India Bill."—Thus the virtues, that could not be difputed, and, which, of all others, are the beft qualifications for a

Britifh

Britifh Minifter, are infidioufly applauded,
merely to ufher in their condemnation by a
fordid return to popular error, and a low
fubmiffion to exploded prejudice.

With equal *impartiality*, with equal
candour, is the portrait of Lord North ex-
hibited—After a picture moft juftly, moft
accurately, moft faithfully delineated, of
the difpofition, the feelings, the heart of
that Minifter; after admitting every beneficent, every humane, every amiable virtue; it would feem unaccountable incon-
fiftency, (unlefs indeed there were an ample
motive for the paradox); to afcribe to that
very mind, fo formed and fo tempered, the
origin of a war, which, whoever has common rationality, or reflection, *muft know*,
did *not* originate with the " humane, the
" beneficent" Lord North. With whom
that war *did* originate; for what purpofes it

was

was undertaken; with what views inflexibly maintained; is a refearch for Pofterity to eftablifh.—With whomfoever it *did* originate, qualities and difpofitions of indeed a very different defcription muft uniformly have prevailed. Dark, vindictive, unrelenting Cruelty; cold, fullen, untractable perverfenefs; a fyftematic hatred of Liberty; a heavy ignorance of our Laws; a malignant perverfion of our Conftitution. That a miftaken fenfe of perfonal Honour, fo long retained Lord North in the faithful, but ignoble fituation of an inftrument of State, was a conduct not all the " boafted " Bounty of a Court,*" could poffibly repay; that the moment Lord North both thought, and acted from his own honeft Principles, he fhould be profcribed that Drawing Room, where he

* Review, page 39.

fo

fo long had ferved, is at once a leffon to mifplaced attachment, and a monument of Regal Gratitude.

I do not follow the precife order which *The Review* has marfhalled out for examining the various Characters it delineates. There is one part of it, to which I referve my laft obfervations. Were I to indulge the feelings which are excited in every generous mind, by the fhameful attack on the Prince of Wales, how were it poffible to turn to the lighter parts of this work, with the fort of temper they are properly entitled to ?

There is fomething fo uncommonly pleafant, though puzzling, in the quadruple parallels of Themiftocles and Phocion, of Scipio and Camillus, to Lord Rodney and Mr. Haftings, that it wonderfully relieves

the

the imagination, and refreshes the fancy, in the midst of more serious thoughts, to develope the resemblances of such extraordinary comparisons, and to calculate to which of the modern Heroes, the respective virtues of the ancient are to be appropriated; or whether indeed the total merits of the antique models are not to go in the aggregate to each of the living Examples.

Before, however, I become the modern Plutarch between Greeks, Romans, and Englishmen, I beg leave to protest against any serious junction of Lord Rodney's and Mr. Hastings's characters. However I may object to parts of the former's conduct, I hold him as much above the latter, as practical bravery is superior to speculative rashness. The one drew his sword, to support the public cause—the other merely his pen, to satiate his private enmities. Such an Admiral

ral in his Hammock, and such a Governor
in his Palanquin, are as widely diffimilar as
the fea and land; and furely the leaft partial
devotee of Rodney would fpurn at the comparifon.

But let us turn to antiquity. " Themif-
" tocles, the Admiral of Athens, was
" faid to have a fword, but no heart*"—fo
far the *Grecian* ftory might feem exclufively
a naval precedent—But, fays the fame
Plutarch, " Three beautiful Captives, allied
" to the royal blood, were feized by The-
" miftocles himfelf, and facrificed, in their
" fplendid Vefts of Gold, to Bacchus, the
" Devourer." An example not lefs illuf-
trated by the plunder of female dignity,
and the pillage of princely victims, in
Oude.

* Plutarch.

† Id.

Of

Of Phocion it is recorded, that " Alex-
" ander having affigned him a prefent of a
" hundred Talents, that excellent Greek
" rejeſted the munificent largefs with a
" modeſt, but firm equanimity," giving
(fays the hiſtorian) an illuſtrious example,
" how rich that man is, who, by contraſting
" his mind, has no occafion for more."
How difficult, how arduous to afcertain,
who moſt is entitled to fuch a parallel ; the
great Oriental acceptor of prohibited prefents,
or the bold inſtigator of unlicenfed pillage !

But what increafes the dilemma, is the
charaſter and the conduſt of the *Wife* of
Phocion. — " A matron," fays Plutarch,
" of no lefs reputation among the Athenians
" for virtue and good houfewifery, than
" Phocion was for probity—Attir'd in a
" modeſt and fimple habit," fays the
Hiſtorian, " did this plain lady reprove a

* Id.

D   " ſtrange

" ftrange dame of Ionia, who difplayed her
" golden embroidery, her jewels, her brace-
" lets, and her necklaces," — " For my
" part, Madam," faid the modeft matron,
" all *my* ornament is my good man Pho-
" cion!"—A fentiment fo equally conform-
able to each of the adduced parallels of
either fex, as really to leave the mind in
complete fufpence, on whom the fimilitude
can moft juftly be beftowed.

" Non noftrum eft tantas componere lites:
" Et vitulâ tu dignus & hic."——

But now as to the third comparifon.——
" When the ancient city of Veii was ftormed,
" and the foldiers were bufied in pillaging,
" and gathering riches and fpoils, Camillus
" from a lofty tower, beheld it and wept*."
—How applicable to the mild conqueror of

* Plutarch's life of Camillus.

Benares! yet how equally a parallel to the humanity of the Euftatia triumph! But Camillus, it feems, defrauded his foldiers of a portion of their fpoils—✝ Say, ye Eaftern armies ; fay, ye Weftern fleets, which of your conductors has beft fuftained his claffick model ?—

It is fortunate however that, in the laft fimilitude, a diftinct Scipio may fairly be allotted to both the competitors. The honours of *Afiaticus* can fcarcely be difputed —The name, the conduct, and the fortune, are equally appropriated; for Afiaticus was not only impeached, but condemned by the ftate ✝, for embezzling four million of fefterces ‡, received in Afia on the publick account. — *Africanus*, however, deferved

✝ Id.
‡ Livy.
§ Review.

D 2   and

and gained a better fate. By the advice of
Cato, it was moved in the Senate, that he
fhould give an account of the fpoils he had
taken in the war with Antiochus—he could
not, however, be formally arraigned or
abfolved, becaufe *his papers,* " *the effential*
" *vouchers*§, *were deftroyed* "—But the bat-
tle of Zama was his defence, and a grateful
people accepted the plea.—

I fear I have wandered too widely on the
fertile eminences of claffick heroifm ; I de-
fcend with humbled thoughts,

   " To the fubjected plain——·
   " With dreadful faces throng'd, and fiery arms."

I will not wound the high feeling of
Lord Rodney's mind, by one ferious refuta-
tion of a comparifon between *his* brave and
manly character, however tinged or dif-
coloured by a tranfient cloud of Avarice; and
that

that of a *Civil* Commander, whofe whole
adminiftration is at this moment delibe-
rately and folemnly charged with Pecula-
tion, with Oppreffion, with Violation of
Treaty; with the dethroning of Sovereigns,
the defolation of Provinces, and the extir-
pation of Nations.—God forbid, that a
Culprit arraigned for fo black a mafs of
enormous offence, fhould for a moment be
prejudged!—It is true he is charged with thofe
delinquencies by a man of undifputed knowledge, and unfufpected integrity.—Of one
of the moft malignant of thofe delinquencies
he is already judged to be apparently guilty.
—May the juftice, but the merciful juftice,
of his Country revolve the various feries
of his actions, with a deep and confcientious
attention to the character, and the honour
of the Englifh name; but with a mild and
lenient recollection of the weaknefs and frail-
ty of human nature. Such be the ultimate
decifion

decifion on Mr. Haftings.—But let not his name, at *this* moment, be blended with Lord Rodney's!— If even the unworthy have been *illegally* deprived of their ill-got wealth, let the whole be fcrupuloufly reftored.—— But let National Gratitude give cafe, give opulence, to their brave officer, and recompence to his gallant companions—What the fpirit of Ireland beftowed on the Champion of her Conftitution, let the juftice of England render to the protector of her Sovereignty—And, if the plodding penury of one narrow mind ftart at the profufion, let his Grace of Richmond be told, it was not the *Expence* of his ridiculous whims that revolted againft the judgement of a Britifh Houfe of Commons. The very men who moft oppofed that filly extravagance, would ftand foremoft in a liberal vote for the fuppport and the honour of our Navy.

Amid

Amid the exercise of perfonal reflection, the little manual of St. James's interfperfes a few elementary attempts at poetical and political Criticifm.—The Beauties of the Rolliad, and the Graces of the Commercial Treaty, are introduced as a fort of *entremets* in the pleafant banquet that regales the nice tafte and faftidious appetites of its Courtly Guefts. The great fubftantial difhes require a judicious mixture of lighter dainties: and efpecially, after a hot *Curry,* the pretty trifling of the fecond courfe, and the cracking a few literary walnuts and edifying cherries, in queft of interleaved mottoes; or the fipping a little of Mr. Eden's frothed cream; are delicate relaxations from the fatigues of venifon: while the two Secretaries of State are juft collaterally mentioned, like the cold things on the fide table—and the Chancellor and Lord Hawkefbury referved as a

Devil'd

Devil'd Gizzard, and a dried Herring, by way of *bonne bouche*, before the defert.

It is no very aufpicious prefage of political judgement, to betray a fhallownefs of Critical Tafte.—The Review is profufe of general applaufe on *Rolliads* and *Odes.* But then, what fignificant apprehenfions, that all their beft points muft fink into obfcurity, as rapidly as the perfonalities of the Dunciad: or, in other words, that General Political Satire is juft as perifhable, as temporary Attack on obfcure Scribblers and Bookfellers, who were fcarcely known in their day.

Thus weak on Literature, let us try the Reviewer on ferious, fober bufinefs: the Commercial Treaty. Firft, " It is pregnant, (he fafely obferves) with unknown " benefits, or—injuries." " It's a complete " Revolution

" Revolution ; but—only an experiment.*"
" It departs from all the policy of paſt
" ages; it is complicate, intricate; yet *muſt*
" be regarded with predilection*." But
above all, he adds, " The People of Eng-
" land will act as ignorant, credulous
" dupes, unleſs they *accept* the *preſent*
" Treaty ; becauſe it bears an intimate
" reſemblance to the *former*, which they
" rejected." And then " It's ſo mild an
" interchange," * " and ſo reciprocal," *
" and ſo unlike" " thoſe illiberal, *devaſting*
" wars." *

　" With many holiday and lady terms,
　" Talking ſo like a waiting gentlewoman,
　" Of drums and guns and wounds—God ſave the
　　　" mark,—
　" And that 'twas great pity, ſo it was,
　" That villainous ſalt-petre ſhould be digg'd
　" Out of the bowels of the harmleſs earth—
　" And all that bald, unjointed chat."

—For pity's fake, to what are we to attribute this exceſſive flimſineſs, even to drivelling, in our Courtly Reviewer; and on a ſubject too, where a ſudden and unprecedented attempt to ſacrifice all the high views and principles, that for ages have dignified and exalted our national character, already appears to have awakened and alarmed the feelings of every liberal and diſintereſted character in the kingdom.

> " Diſſentientes conditionibus
> " Fœdis & exempio trahenti
> " Perniciem, veniens in avum."

—But poſſibly the Reviewer has thought it unfair to Mr. Roſe to anticipate that true ſort of lumping, bulky, cumberfome, Commercial Pamphlet, which the unpreſuming Secretary is preparing on the French Treaty, as a companion to his Defence of the Iriſh Propoſitions.——What a happy proſpect of ample atonement for this

firſt

firſt frivolous Defence of the Treaty by the
Reviewer! We now can look forward to a
real, ſubſtantial, ſolid, unwieldy Tract; ſtuff-
ed with all the erudition of an Exciſeman;
and interlarded with Dictionary ſcience, and
garbled Reports; where the grand ſubjects
too are arranged, like the various ſtrata of
the earth!

On the external cruſt, animal and vege-
table documents;

W O O L.

C O T T O N.

H O P S.

F L A X.

H E M P!

In the intermediate regions, leſs ſuper-
ficial and more ſolid matter;

FULLER'S EARTH!

C O A L!

In the still inferior, with due respect to
gravitation, the heavier masses of mineral
and metallick information;

COPPER

IRON

BRASS!

It would indeed have proved a most irk-
some talk to a polite writer, to encroach on a
toil so properly allotted to patient dullness;
—for how few are there who have the me-
chanick industry to turn out, like the Scotch
Pedlars of Commercial Composition, with
their pack of petty assortments ; their Shef-
field scissars, and their Birmingham buttons?
Every leaf of these motley compositions
displays an epitome of all the tricks of in-
vitation, that are practised by the trades they
discuss; some of them intoxicating the eye,
like Vintners' windows, with BRANDY!
RUM! and BRITISH SPIRIT! in
capitals—

capitals—while others denote their beaten
track, and towns of baiting; like the letter-
ed pannels of a ſtage coach, in characters
of a moſt extenſive and convincing ſize;
as,

HULL,	BOCKING,
LEEDS,	BRAINTREE,
WAKEFIELD, ᵒʳ	DUNMOW,
YORK,	COLCHESTER,&c.

It has been well ſaid, that, on ſuch topicks,
A Warehouſe is more uſeful than a Li-
brary, and a Clothier a better authority than a Claſſick.——Leaving therefore the ſilly and the ſtupid equally to
oblivion; let us turn to loftier or to gentler
themes; the combined laurels of the im-
mortal Frederick, or the milder olive of a
domeſtick Sovereign.

Incomparable in the ſelection of ancient
parallels

parallels, with what equal perfpicuity has
the pleafant writer of the Court Review
connected two mighty Monarchs, of modern date, in one little Pamphlet! With an
excurfive flattery, that bounds from the ram-
part of Potfdam to the Caftle Ditch at
Windfor; with a digreffive fervility that at
one moment, mopes over the State Tomb at
Rerlin; the next, wearies the tutelary Gods
f Britain with Tory Thankfgivings?---
what talents, what tafte, what feelings
muft he poffefs, to render fuch ingenious
homage, both to dead and living Royalty!
—How gracefully does he ftrew the Pruffian
Grave with deathlefs flowers! " Splendour
" of talents"*—" Every fublime endow-
" ment of the human mind"†--"graced with
" both Minervas," ‡ " with unexampled
" difplay of military prowefs, and civil

* Review, p. 50.
† Page 51.
‡ Page 53.

" wif-

" wifdom,"§ " he fecured, he *extended* his
" dominions ,"‖ " the protector of van-
" quifhed enemies." " Clement and for-
" giving even to injuries moft wounding."
" Courted and admired throughout Europe
" by its Princes."

Such are the pure fources of no cafual
popularity.—The fame of *Frederick* is not
fabricated on the rotten foundation of
the faults or follies of others.—Childlefs
as Charles the 2d, or William the 3d*, the
King of Pruffia was not protected by the
name of father, or of hufband †. — *He* did
not, even after repeated defeats, and in the
midft of a difaftrous war, when his armies
were flaughtered, and his fubjects' lands laid
wafte by the enemy; *he* did not fly from

§ Review, p. 5.
‖ Id. p. 6.
* Review.
† Id.

3   perils,

perils, (fomewhat greater than a mob of boys could menace,) like the good uxurious Priam, to the protecting arms of Hecuba, and her diffufive offspring.—Still lefs did this incautious Hero plant batteries in his park, or furround his Palace with a triple camp.

Let us paufe, before we touch on the fucceeding portion of this Royal comparifon —let us paufe, to indulge fome honeft warmth, againft the weaknefs, the wickednefs, the criminal ineptitude, of that mean and miferable band; who, falfely denominated the *Friends* of Majefty, and who, meafuring the Royal feelings, by the miferable medium of their own, have prefumed to inftigate the friends of Mr. Haftings, to a mixture of the names and characters of the firft in rank and virtue, with the difreputable fubject of India politics, and the fallen caufe of a rafh, prefumptuous man.

To what, but this mixture of the foolish Runners, and dependants on Mr. Haftings, can we attribute the whole of a compofition, the direct object of which is evidently to lower *every* name to the level of Mr. Haftings's; and with perverfe, foolifh malice, to addrefs that fpecies of flattery to His Majefty, which of all others muft wound his feelings moft feverely : that bafe flattery of; not indeed advancing the royal name, or even doing juftice to it ; on the contrary, of infinitely hurting it, by ftrange and ridiculous comparifons; but of detracting from the fenfe, the principle, the honour of the Prince of Wales's name, as an acceptable facrifice to unaccountable jealoufy — Yet, that fuch has been *their* conception, is plain, from every page of the compofition we have criticifed. —To foment an unhappy divifion in the Royal Family—To fcatter unwarrantable doubts among the People—To in-

F   finuate

finuate vifionary apprehenfions—To give an idea of a connection impracticable in law, contradictory to the fpirit of the Conftitution, and which to dream of realizing were madnefs, or idiotifm. — That fuch has been the genuine motives of this infidious attempt, is fairly deducible from a plain, candid examination of the whole of *the Court Pamphlet* ; not of *The Court* in its proper fenfe,—but of the vermin of the Court, — of the fawning, flattering fools, who are of more prejudice to their Royal Mafter, than hofts of bold opponents, and open difapprovers.

Confider for a moment this fenfelefs attempt at Royal Panegyrick—What is the amount of the praifes prepared for His Majefty ?——Firft, in lieu of the loft Colonies, there are nearly as many Royal Children — and then, allayed by domeftick

meftick continence and decorum alone, burft forth " deftructive councils *," — " accu- " mulated taxes *," — " difgrace abroad *," " diftrefs at home *," — " political infigni- " ficance entailed on a degraded King- " dom *." All thefe are fummed up, even rhetorically, on the debtor fide. —— And what is the credit, *per contra ?*—Why, firft of all, " His Majefty is a married man * ;— then he has a fine family" *—and a curious picture is drawn of a moralizing mob † refting on their bludgeons, to defcant on thefe pious themes, and at laft philofophical- ly refolving not to break the palace windows; —becaufe their fovereign —had a wife and children *.

Next, the Coalition is another great auxiliary fupport * of the King's popu- larity—Lord North and Mr. Fox fhook

* Review.

hands,

hands, and right or wrong, that recon=
ciliation made the King popular.—

Thirdly, the India bill was a very bad
bill, and therefore the King grew more
popular.—

Fourthly, a mad woman put a defert knife
in a fheet of paper, and held out both to
the King, and that made the King more and
more popular.*—and two or three Towns
began addreffing, and then every other
Town could not but addrefs too—to the
violent increafe of the King's popularity*.

But laft, and above all, the Prince of
Wales grew unpopular, and therefore his
Father got all the popularity he loft—*

Thus—on the one hand, pofitive mifcon-
duct

* Review

duct and fubftantial misfortune, backed with
the Subject's diftrefs, and the Country's dif-
honour, are directly imputed as the *fhades*
of character — and tolerably gloomy they
are---while the *lights* are pale and feeble indeed, and moft of them cold and dim as
Moonfhine — mere negative virtues in the
poffeffor---propped on the fuppofed depra-
vity of others—on a cafualty—on Corpo-
ration compliments—a mad Millener—and
a giddy Prince.

Now it is plain this laft was confidered
as the great point to urge — from a ridiculous conception entertained by the writer
and his abfurd advifers, that there is a fort
of policy in all Sovereigns to deprefs their
apparent Succeffors. — That fuch a policy
but too frequently exifted in defpotick con-
ftitutions may be vouched by hiftory—Phi-
lip the Second of Spain, whofe perverfe and
ignorant

ignorant ambition fent the Duke d'Alva to
force taxation on his Colonies with the
bayonet and the rack, and who loft them
by the mad attempt; in hatred of his Son
Don Carlos, and of that imprudent predilection for liberty, which the Prince had
avowed ; firft traduced and oppreffed the ill-
fated Youth, by falfe accufations and a fuborn-
ed condemnation; then legally murdered him.
But wherefore recur to any diftant Period for
Examples of the Jealoufy of defpotick
Princes againft thofe who are prefently hateful
to them, becaufe, even in future, and when,
in the courfe of Nature they are to be no
more, their followers may ultimately be as
great as themfelves. The wretched Jea-
loufies of Afiatick Defpotifm are innume-
rable. In exact proportion as the Prince is
graced with every Quality that properly
diftinguifhes his Rank; in proportion as he
is fpirited, liberal, munificent, attractive
by

by his Perfon and his Manners; in juft an
equal degree he becomes odious to the
gloomy Tyrant of the Seraglio.—The
Mutes nod away his character —the Bow-
ftring terminates his life—Nor has the
defpotifm of modern Europe (for where
has the ambition of France left a fpark of
Liberty but in England?) appeared lefs
generaliy, though operating with more cautious and more difcreet feverity.—The late
Emprefs of Germany kept her fon as a State
Pauper, to make him obedient to her own
caprice, and a flave to the Monks, whom
fhe enriched at his expence.—Circumftan-
ces are a little inverted at prefent.—What
bigotry withheld or mifapplied, has rigidly
been reclaimed by the edicts of a clever
Man ftarved into a Reformer.—What Chains
of Penury were faftened even on the Prince
of Pruffia, by his Mighty Predeceffor!—
How far the *paft* reftraints on the gallantry of

that

that Monarch may have produced a multi-
plicity of *prefent* Amours, is an unfair inquiry
—but certainly His Majefty of Pruffia was
too poor to have a Miftrefs *before* He afcend-
ed his Throne—In Ruffia, the tender ex-
penditures of Imperial *patronage* may be
fome excufe for the diftreffes in which the
grand Duke and Duchefs are retained.
Where a Sovereign, who has a tafte for va-
riety, prefides, the only man in her dominions,
who muft defpair of her munificence, is he
who has the honour, but ill fortune, to be
too nearly her relation.—In Spain, the
Prince of Afturias, with all his fpirited
and manly feelings, has long been in fubjec-
tion to poverty;—the admired yet neglected
victim of jealoufy and weaknefs.—But not
one of thefe precedents, except in the minds
of traitors or of fools, can fupply the flight-
eft ground of imitation in the free conftitution of England—under the moderate power

of

of a limited Monarch, the very tenure of its prefcribed authority; the public laws which define, and reftrain its extent, and, above all, the general Spirit of a National character, that *will* circumfcribe its operations ; all appeal to the wifdom and the feelings of the fupreme Magiftrate of fuch a State, to quell every meddling wifh, to fubdue every fecret propenfity, that leads to the dangerous heights of inordinate ambition.—Such a Monarch will learn to eftimate the direction of a free People, as a great and facred truft deputed to him for the beft and nobleft purpofes; and to the laft refignation of which, he may look forward with the fame mild complacency, that private life revolves the fucceffion of a wellufed patrimony.—Who then is that infidious malignant, that has prefumed to publifh to the world, that, the hope of a future age has " departed from that filial piety

G   " and

" and obedience ;" * which nature, which duty, which, above all, a father's virtues demand, and deferve ?

Let us recall a few facts, plain, and undifputed.

Notwithftanding the flight domeftick dif-fention, which unfortunately had fubfifted for fome time ; what was His Royal Highnefs's fenfe of filial affection, on the firft rumour of the King's danger ? Without a moment's delay, he haftened to throw himfelf at His Majefty's feet.—It is in the knowledge of every one, that His Royal Highnefs was *not* admitted to the Royal Prefence.——
The neceffity for providing a proper refi-dence at Carleton Houfe, augmented the expenditure of the Prince.—The difficulty

Review.

was

was ſtated with every poſſible reſpect. No
redreſs was afforded. —

The revenues of the Dutchy of Cornwall
veſt in a Prince of Wales the moment of his
birth—On the loweſt poſſible eſtimate, the
annual receipts are 10,000£. a year. The
accumulation of theſe profits during the courſe
of His Royal Highneſs's minority, amount
to a ſum much more than ſufficient to cancel
the incurred debt. If the Prince had humbly
ſolicited the payment of that ſum, on
grounds unqueſtionably legal, it is ſcarcely
poſſible that the common ties of parent and
child, or the general principle of Mainte-
nance could have been held leſs binding on
the higheſt, than on all the other ranks of
ſociety. Nor do the various grants, that
Parliament, from time to time, moſt liberally
provided for every poſſible increaſe of the
civil expenditure, leave a ground for ſuppo-

ſing.

fing, that the revenue of the Prince could be
ftated as applied and appropriated to the purpofes of education during his Highnefs' mi-
nority-—Yet a requifition of what never
was *offered*, however fanctioned by juftice,
law, and almoft neceffity, might, poffibly,
have been mifconftrued into offence.—The
claim, therefore, *never* was made. —

May we not inquire then, to which part of
thefe inftances, the character of a " a Depar-
" ture from the facred and primeval laws of
" nature" is to be affixed ?—Or from what
bofom we are to deplore the abfence of " na-
" tural and kindly affections ?"*—Do they
contain a trace, a fhadow of " *filial* impiety
and difobedience ? " *   Or do any other inftances exift of a neglect of *filial* duty ?

* Revew, p. 17.

Deprived

Deprived of a proper refidence, and fenfible of the irkfome fituation of continuing in fo unfuitable an appearance as the neceffary dif-miffion of his houfehold muft occafion, it was his Highnefs's wifh to go abroad. — His Majefty's difapprobation of the purpofe was fuggefted; — and inftantly that fuggeftion was obeyed as a command. —

All England, all Europe, are acquainted with the voluntary appropriations made by his Highnefs of more than half of his income, to the gradual payment of the increafed debt.

Neither the common fenfe nor the natural feeling of the reader fhall be infulted with a fingle comment on fuch a facrifice. —

As for the dark infinuation of an ambigu-ous *Connection*; though already adverted to, it cannot be too often or too plainly refuted,

by

by this direct, unequivocal anfwer; that the
Laws and Conftitution of England muft be
annihilated, before a union of that nature
can poffibly take place; both the fpirit and
the letter of our ftatutes confronting, op-
pofing, and repelling it, by fixed and infur-
mountable barriers.

Having lodged this folemn, and explicit
anfwer to the ungenerous, and unmanly
infinuations that have bafely been diffemi-
nated on this fubject, I might inquire
with what confiftency thofe very fame
" impoifoned arrows," * which are con-
traband even for Wit to carry to Kew or
Windfor, become articles of open trade, and
free of all duty, in the dulleft adventure
againft Carleton Houfe?—Its " unfair, * un-
" dignified, ‡ ungenerous perfonality;" to
hunt out " the little weaknefs infeparable

* Review.

from

" from mortality,"—if a King's in ques-
tion—" *Such divinity doth hedge a King!*"—
But to afperfe, to malign, to falfify a Prince,
is merely a fort of petty Treafon, for which
it may not be impoffible to obtain a Nolo
Profequi, or even a pardon.—I might too
inquire, how a Gentleman, who, with very
ufeful candour, confeffes he has never been
admitted to the Prince's prefence, can
reafonably proclaim himfelf the Cenfor of
His Royal Highnefs's fociety.—That every
man of the moft approved abilities, of the
moft refined wit, of the moft elegant manners, was felected by the Prince, as the beft
honour of his table, (while He had one,) can
only be unknown to fuch, whofe conftitu-
tional habits of treachery, (a defcription,
poffibly not ambiguous, or indefinite to the
Reviewer,) have marked them out, as the
moft dangerous, and the moft unworthy
affociates, either in public or private life.—

In

In a society, where those whose respectability and excellence of character even
the Court Pamphlet has admitted; and where
too even a few of the present Ministers have
not unfrequently appeared, either from untramelled taste, or as spies;—the quick, observing talents, the familiar, yet never unguarded manners, of an accomplished mind,
have indicated every hereditary quality that
could be wished for, and, (is it necessary to
add ?) have unequivocally denoted the manners of a gentleman, and the spirit of a man of
honour.—To the guests of Carleton House,
the Portlands, the Fitzwilliams, (the Rockinghams of their day;) to the ready talents,
that can turn from politicks to poetry, from
a debate to criticism, from argument to wit,
in a word, to all the versatile faculties and
powers of Mr. Fox, Mr. Sheridan, Mr.
Erskine, Mr. Hare, Mr. Fitzpatrick — to
these, and to the judgement and taste that

can

can select, and relish such companions, are opposed, by the good-natured spirit of the Review, the casual toleration of some two or three couple of would-be Jesters, and volunteer *Macaros*; who, by virtue of a most adhesive perseverance, and hard-trotting horses, *will* sidle to the Prince in Hyde Park, or pester him at Newmarket.

That any serious objection can exist in a rational mind on such ridiculous grounds, is scarcely more absurd than the curious lamentation of the Court Pamphlet, that His Royal Highness, in these degenerate times, will scarcely become so warlike, or appear so redoubtable, as Henry of Agincourt.—An alarm which really it is not easy to overcome during a general Peace; and when, unluckily too, there remain neither Rebels in America, nor Irish Volunteers, to allure the mind to study Tacticks in General Fawcett's

H   " *Essay*

" *Essay on Salutes,*" or Sir George How-
ard's Converfation. — But it muft partly
remove our concern on this fubject, to
reflect, that, as henceforward we are to
become a *trading* Nation, it might much
interrupt the growing amity of France, if
in any degree we recurred to fuch obfolete
and unpleafant precedents of Military feats.
— Poffibly therefore, fince His Majefty's
Minifters may not have any immediate occafion to roufe the feelings of ancient days,
they may think it wifer, as well as more
difcreet, in future, not openly to encourage
any very violent Libels, either on the honour of a beloved and injured Prince, or
the fenfe and fpirit of a brave, though oppreffed, People.

T H E   E N D.